Lerner SPORTS

ALL-STAR SMACKDOWN

RONALD ACUÑA JR. VS. RICKEY HENDERSON

WHO WOULD WIN?

BRIANNA KAISER

Lerner Publications ◆ Minneapolis

Lerner Publications Company
An imprint of Lerner Publishing Group, Inc.
241 First Avenue North
Minneapolis, MN 55401 USA

For reading levels and more information, look up this title at www.lernerbooks.com.

Main body text set in Aptifer Sans LT Pro.
Typeface provided by Linotype AG.

Editor: Angel Kidd **Designer: Photo Editor:** Angel Kidd

Library of Congress Cataloging-in-Publication Data

Names: Kaiser, Brianna, 1996– author.
Title: Ronald Acuña Jr. vs. Rickey Henderson : who would win? / Brianna Kaiser.
Other titles: Ronald Acuña Junior versus Rickey Henderson
Description: Minneapolis : Lerner Publications, [2025] | Series: Lerner sports. All-star smackdown | Includes bibliographical references and index. | Audience: Ages 7–11 years | Audience: Grades 2–3 | Summary: "Ronald Acuña Jr. and Rickey Henderson are both quick all-star outfielders known for stealing bases. Compare their awards and stats to find out who comes out on top in this MLB face-off!"— Provided by publisher.
Identifiers: LCCN 2024005954 (print) | LCCN 2024005955 (ebook) | ISBN 9798765648254 (lib. bdg.) | ISBN 9798765653197 (epub)
Subjects: LCSH: Baseball players—Rating of—United States—Juvenile literature. | Outfielders (Baseball)—United States—Juvenile literature. | Acuña, Ronald, Jr., 1997—-Juvenile literature. | Henderson, Rickey, 1958—-Juvenile literature. | Sports rivalries—United States—History—Juvenile literature.
Classification: LCC GV865.A1 K325 2024 (print) | LCC GV865.A1 (ebook) | DDC 796.357092/2—dc23/eng/20240401

LC record available at https://lccn.loc.gov/2024005954
LC ebook record available at https://lccn.loc.gov/2024005955

ISBN 979-8-7656-6141-3 (pbk.)

Manufactured in the United States of America
1-1010828-53383-6/11/2024

TABLE OF CONTENTS

Rickey Henderson

INTRODUCTION

RECORDS AND FIRSTS

On May 1, 1991, Rickey Henderson and the Oakland Athletics faced the New York Yankees. Henderson stood on second base, waiting for the right moment to steal third base. Then he took off.

Fast Facts

- Rickey Henderson led the American League (AL) in stolen bases 12 times.
- Henderson won the World Series in 1989 and 1993.
- Ronald Acuña Jr. was the 2023 National League (NL) Most Valuable Player (MVP).
- In 2023, Acuña became the first player to hit at least 40 home runs and steal 70 or more bases in a season.

Henderson sprinted as fast as he could toward third base before sliding in headfirst. The Yankees third baseman Randy Velarde tried to tag out Henderson. But Henderson reached the base first. Safe!

Henderson picked up the base and waved it over his head. The crowd roared with excitement. The amazing moment was Henderson's 939th stolen base of his career. Lou Brock previously held the Major League Baseball (MLB) stolen bases record with 938. Henderson was now the new record holder.

Ronald Acuña Jr. of the Atlanta Braves stepped up to the plate on August 31, 2023. He had teammates on all three bases. When Lance Lynn of the Los Angeles Dodgers threw his pitch, Acuña was ready. *Smack!* Acuña hit a grand slam to give the Braves four runs.

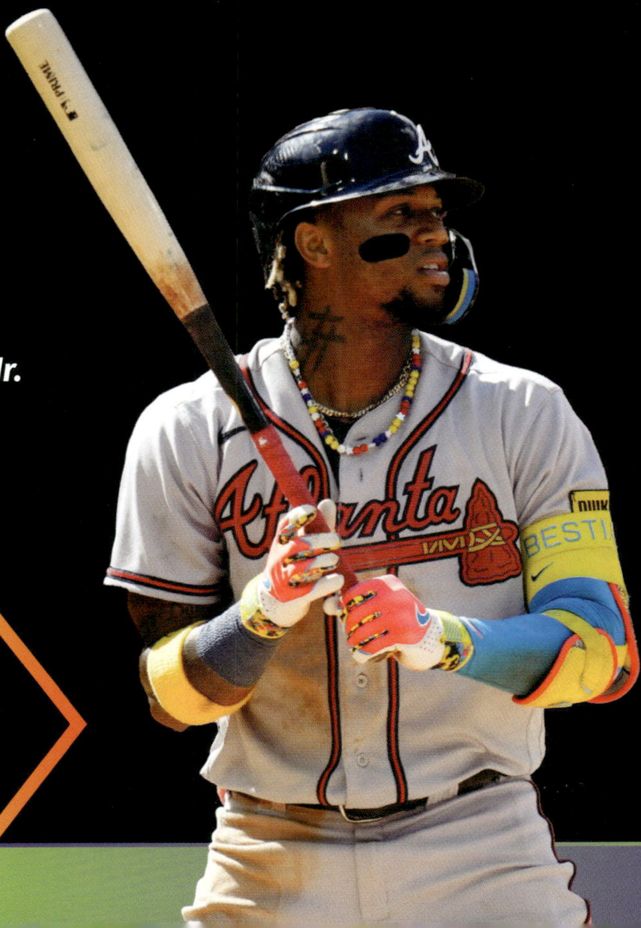

Ronald Acuña Jr.

Acuña's amazing grand slam was his 30th home run of the season. And he had already stolen more than 60 bases that year. Acuña became the first player in MLB history to have at least 30 home runs and 60 stolen bases in the same season.

Both Henderson and Acuña are great at stealing bases. They are also both outfielders. This position is important for a team's defense. Outfielders run down long hits and have the skills to quickly throw the ball back to the infield. But is Henderson or Acuña the better player? Let the smackdown begin!

Henderson dives for his 939th stolen base on May 1, 1991.

Acuña runs up the first base line in the August 31, 2023, game against the Dodgers.

CHAPTER 1

Henderson gets ready to bat during the 1989 World Series.

PATH TO THE PROS

Rickey Henderson was born on December 25, 1958. He grew up in Oakland, California. Rickey played both baseball and football in high school. He was a star running back, but he turned down offers to play college football so he could focus on baseball.

MLB teams take turns choosing new players each year during the MLB Draft. In the 1976 draft, the Oakland Athletics picked Henderson in the fourth round. He played for their minor league teams for four seasons.

Henderson played his first MLB game in 1979. The 20-year-old finished his rookie season with 33 stolen bases. The next season, he stole 100 bases. At the time, he was just one of three players to have stolen 100 or more bases in a season. And it was the first of seven years in a row that Henderson led the AL in stolen bases.

Henderson slides for home plate in a 1979 game against the Baltimore Orioles.

Ronald Acuña Jr. was born on December 18, 1997, in La Guaira, Venezuela. His parents are Ronald Acuña Sr. and Leonelis Blanco. Ronald Jr. began watching and playing baseball at an early age.

Ronald grew up in a family of baseball players. His grandfather Romualdo Blanco, his cousin Jose Campos, and his father all played minor league baseball. His uncle José Escobar and his cousins Alcides, Kelvim, and Edwin Escobar all played major league baseball.

Acuña played his first MLB game on April 25, 2018, with the Atlanta Braves.

Acuña watches the ball fly in his first MLB game.

The St. Louis Cardinals catcher (right) reaches to tag Acuña, who slides home in a 2018 game.

In 2014, 16-year-old Ronald signed a contract with the Atlanta Braves. He worked his way through their minor league teams for a few years. He was 20 when he played his first MLB game on April 25, 2018.

CONSIDER THIS

When Acuña signed with the Braves in 2014, his contract was for $100,000. The best pro baseball players make much more than that. In 2019, Acuña signed a new contract with the Braves for $100 million.

In his rookie season, Acuña became the youngest player to hit home runs for five games in a row. He finished the season with 26 home runs and 16 stolen bases. He was also named the NL Rookie of the Year.

Acuña has always had a knack for hitting homers and stealing bases.

CHAPTER 2

Henderson points toward the stands after hitting a first-inning home run in Game 4 of the 1989 World Series.

GREAT MOMENTS

The World Series is the biggest event in pro baseball. Once a year, the best AL team faces the best NL team. The winner becomes the MLB champion.

At the 1989 World Series, Henderson and the Athletics faced the San Francisco Giants. They beat the Giants in Games 1, 2, and 3. Henderson was the first at bat during Game 4. He was ready for the pitch. *Whack!* His home run helped the Athletics win Game 4 and the World Series.

In 1990, Henderson had one of his top seasons. He led the league in runs scored, stolen bases, and on-base percentage. His 893rd career steal set the AL stolen base record. For his great playing, he was named the AL MVP.

Henderson (left) and Oakland teammates hoist the 1989 World Series trophy.

Acuña runs to third base in a 2019 game against the Pittsburgh Pirates.

Being a member of the 30–30 club is a big deal in pro baseball. Players of the club have hit at least 30 home runs and stolen at least 30 bases in a season. It's even harder to become a member of the 40–40 club.

On September 19, 2019, Acuña joined the 40–30 club. He finished the season with 41 home runs and 37 stolen bases. Acuña played even better in 2023. On August 31, he hit his grand slam to bring him to 30 home runs and 61 stolen bases for the season. Then, on September 22, he hit his 40th home run of the season. The home run made him the fifth player in MLB history to join the 40–40 club.

Acuña hits a triple in the first inning of a 2019 game.

Five days later, Acuña had the greatest moment of his career. In a game against the Chicago Cubs, he stole his 70th base of the season. He became the first player to ever join the 40–70 club. He finished the season with 41 home runs and 73 stolen bases, and he won the NL MVP award.

Acuña holds up second base after stealing it on September 27, 2023. It was his 70th steal of the season.

Acuña plays right field in a 2021 game.

CONSIDER THIS

There are three outfield positions. They are left fielder, center fielder, and right fielder. Henderson mainly played as a left fielder. Acuña has played all outfield positions, but he prefers to play right fielder.

CHAPTER 3

Henderson wins the MVP trophy for the 1989 AL Championship Series.

AWARD WINNERS

Henderson played pro baseball for 25 years. During his long career, he won many awards and set records that may never be broken. Acuña's career is much shorter so far. But he has also won awards and set records in the sport.

Henderson was great at stealing bases. He finished 22 seasons in the AL top 10 for the category. Of those 22 seasons, he led the league in stolen bases 12 times. He finished his career with 1,406 stolen bases, the most in MLB history.

Acuña led the NL in stolen bases in 2019 and 2023. He has fewer career stolen bases than Henderson, but Acuña hit more home runs in the beginning of his career than Henderson did. In his first five seasons, Acuña hit 120 home runs in 514 games. Henderson only hit 35 home runs in 649 games.

Henderson finished his career with 297 home runs and a .279 batting average. He got a hit in almost 28 out of every 100 at bats. By the end of 2023, Acuña already had 161 career home runs and a .292 batting average. He gets a hit in about 29 out of 100 at bats.

Acuña (right) high-fives Eugenio Suárez after Acuña hit a home run in the 2018 MLB Japan All-Star Series.

Each year, the best NL and AL players of that season play in the MLB All-Star Game. The game is played in the middle of the MLB season. Henderson was named to 10 All-Star Games. Acuña has been named to four All-Star Games.

Henderson (left) talks to Boston Red Sox player Carl Yastrzemski (center) before the 1982 All-Star Game.

CONSIDER THIS

A team retires a jersey number to honor the player who wore it. When a number is retired, no other player of that team will ever wear it again. In 2009, the Oakland Athletics retired Henderson's number 24.

Henderson and Acuña are almost equal in the number of other awards they have received. Both players have been league MVPs. Henderson was the AL MVP in 1990, and Acuña was the NL MVP in 2023.

The Silver Slugger Award is given every year to the best hitter at each position in both leagues. Henderson and Acuña have both won the award three times. Acuña also won the NL Hank Aaron Award in 2023. Each year, it is given to the top hitter in each league.

Acuña (center) accepts the 2023 NL Hank Aaron Award.

CHAPTER 4

Acuña hits his 40th home run of the 2023 season, putting him in the 40–40 club.

AND THE WINNER IS

It's time to decide if Henderson or Acuña is the winner of this exciting baseball smackdown. Sports fans may have different opinions. That's all part of the fun. Consider the major achievements of these two players, and see who comes out on top.

Henderson holds the record for most career stolen bases. That record may never be broken. But Acuña has led the league in stolen bases in more than one season. And he became the first and only player to hit at least 40 home runs and steal 70 or more bases in a season.

Henderson runs for a base in a 1990 game.

Henderson won the World Series with the Oakland Athletics in 1989 and again with the Toronto Blue Jays in 1993. In 2021, Acuña played for half of the season before he had a knee injury. Although Acuña had to miss the rest of the season, his playing helped the Braves reach and win the World Series that year. Acuña cheered on his team, but he has yet to play in this major event.

Henderson holds the 1993 World Series trophy.

Acuña grins after scoring the game-winning run against the Chicago Cubs on September 27, 2023.

Henderson had an incredible career. He played his last MLB season in 2003 at the age of 44. In 2009, Henderson joined the National Baseball Hall of Fame. Acuña is still young and likely has many more years to play. If Acuña plays to the age of 44 as Henderson did, he has a chance to break or set many more records. That is why Acuña is the winner of this all-star smackdown.

Now it's your turn. Who do you think the winner is? Think it over, make your choice, and talk about it with a friend!

SMACKDOWN BREAKDOWN

RICKEY HENDERSON

Date of birth: December 25, 1958
Height: 5 feet 10 (1.8 m)
Career home runs: 297
Career batting average: .279
Career stolen bases: 1,406

Stats are accurate through the 2023 MLB season.

RONALD ACUÑA JR.

Date of birth: December 18, 1997
Height: 6 feet (1.8 m)
Career home runs: 161
Career batting average: .292
Career stolen bases: 180

GLOSSARY

All-Star Game: a game played in the middle of each Major League Baseball season with that season's best players

American League (AL): with the National League (NL), one of the two leagues that make up Major League Baseball

at bat: a turn at batting

batting average: a figure calculated by dividing a player's number of hits by their number of times at bat

draft: when teams take turns choosing new players

grand slam: a home run hit with a runner on every base

infield: the area of a baseball field enclosed by the three bases and home plate

Major League Baseball (MLB): the highest level of professional baseball in the US

minor league: a pro baseball league that is not a major league

on-base percentage: a stat that shows how often a batter reaches base by a hit, a walk, or being hit by a pitch

rookie: a first-year player

stolen base: when a runner advances a base without the ball being hit

LEARN MORE

Baseball Hall of Fame: Rickey Henderson
https://baseballhall.org/hall-of-famers/henderson-rickey

Flynn, Brendan. *Atlanta Braves All-Time Greats*. Mendota Heights, MN: Press Box Books, 2021.

MLB: Ronald Acuña Jr.
https://www.mlb.com/player/ronald-acuna-jr-660670

Olson, Ethan. *Great MLB World Series Championships*. San Diego: BrightPoint, 2024.

Schwartz, Heather E. *Meet Ronald Acuña Jr.: Atlanta Braves Superstar.* Minneapolis: Lerner Publications, 2025.

Sports Illustrated Kids: Baseball
https://www.sikids.com/baseball

INDEX

PHOTO ACKNOWLEDGMENTS

Image credits: AP Photo/Chris O'Meara, p. 4; AP Photo/Matt Slocum, p. 5; AP Photo/Eric Risberg, p. 6; AP Photo/Brian Rothmuller/Icon Sportswire, p. 7; AP Photo/NewsBase, pp. 8, 25; AP Photo/James Palmer, p. 9; AP Photo/John Minchillo, pp. 10–11, 13; AP Photo/Jeff Roberson, p. 12; AP Photo/Leonard Ignelzi, p. 14; AP Photo/Paul Sakuma, p. 15; AP Photo/Austin McAfee/Icon Sportswire, p. 16; AP Photo/John Bazemore, p. 17; AP Photo/Rich von Biberstein/Icon Sportswire, pp. 18, 27; AP Photo/Joe Robbins/Icon Sportswire, pp. 19, 29; Jerry Wachter/Sports Illustrated/Getty Images, p. 20; AP Photo/Kyodo, p. 21; AP Photo, p. 22; Daniel Shirey/Getty Images, p. 23; G Fiume/Getty Images, p. 24; John Iacono/Sports Illustrated/Getty Images, p. 26; AP Photo/John Cordes/Icon Sportswire, p. 28.

Cover: AP Photo/Cliff Welch/Icon Sportswire; AP Photo/David Durochik.